A Spiritual Teacher's Notebook

High Thoughts From A Later-Day Master

About: Love • Truth • Universal Consciousness
Space/Time • Subjective Reality
Transformation • God and You

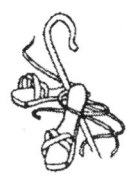

A Spiritual Teachers Notebook: High Thoughts From A Later-Day Master Master Teacher

This Edition Printed, March 2004

International Standard Book Number (ISBN) 1-890648-02-7
Library of Congress Catalog Card Number: PENDING

Published by Endeavor Academy Library
An Imprint of Endeavor Academy
501 East Adams Street, Wisconsin Dells WI, 53965
United States of America

ENDEAVOR ACADEMY
"Certum est quia impossibile est"

And greater works will you do than
I have done...

And the government shall be
upon your shoulders...

To every human being on Earth who, somewhere in space/time, for a single moment, has experienced being completely awakened to his individual, indivisible state of eternal consciousness.

Preface

The time has come on earth for the maturing and emergence of individuals with genuinely expanded ranges of consciousness mind.

Historically humans have described these individuals as masters or avatars or adepts or initiates or even saviors or man-gods.

The accelerated evolution (or even revolution) of mind now in progress on the planet involves the metamorphosis of what can be termed Later-Day Masters.

The material contained herein is representational of the thinking of this sort of new mindedness. It is an absolutely enlightened order of thought.

Face it, the human race is finally going to have to look squarely at the idea of atonement or resurrection or a dramatic shift in self-identity or whatever else you call it.

Listen carefully to me now for we are about to take a crucial step. It is absolutely imperative that you as an individual human being, seriously entertain the possibility that knowledge can be gained by an actual mind transformative process. That you have progressed far enough in your search for self-identity to have this little book in hand is a very excellent indication that you have taken or are about to take this most important step at least intellectually. There will be something very disturbing to you about my assertion with absolute certainty that the very nature of my conceptual thought is different than what is termed here on earth a human being (that is an egoic personality). Indeed, having awakened from the fractured imagery that constitutes earth perception, I am well aware of the disbelief, derision, suspicion and even alarm that can accompany the notion of the emergence of a truly so called supra-consciousness or one that conceives itself from an expanded consciousness state. Conversely, from my awakened status of mind the idea that teachings of singular truth, indivisible wholeness or Godliness and absolute universal order obtained by a process of non-judgment, defenselessness, forgiveness and love is considered by the average human mind to be a threat to its existence from which it must defend itself is pitifully absurd and obviously rank insanity.

Actually, in the framework of space/time I am nothing but an early version of a unity conscious model that will and did become extremely common as a communicator of truth, light, love and harmony to the dark and fearful chaotic self-conceptions that constitute the earth. I have remembered that I am a whole part of the natural state of the universe which is totally and eternally creative with no possibility of separation or opposition. Not incidentally, the original model for all Master Teachers in regard to individual transformation to Spiritual Man or Son of Godship or God-Manhood is Master Brother Jesus Christ of Nazareth. Not only is he the model but indeed, his Sermon on the Mount (Matt 5) is the original catechism of the method to be used to bring about the mind and body transformation of every apparently separated consciousness, to the true conception of self as singular universal truth. Obviously all the method of salvation you could ever, ever need is the practice of "Resist not Evil." This must lead to totally unqualified forgiveness which is finally the simple recognition that nothing real could ever be threatened nor could it be separated from everything, which is what God and Truth is.

If it is true then, that this knowledge of a single identity that is eternal happiness and peace can only be gained through a spiritual maturation or mind transformation, whose mind is it that must change? Listen to me now. I say to you with unqualified certainty that the individual consciousness that finally brought and will bring eternal happiness, peace and love to mankind is and was yours. It could never have happened in any other fashion. As one of these Later-Day Masters, I am absolutely certain of your Divine Brotherhood and Saviorship. Literally, as master of your thoughts, you are Master of the World. Only through your resurrection of mind can the world be saved from the illusion of fear and annihilation.

The Dilemma of a Savior of the World

My awakening to Christhood or Mastership is in its very occurrence a verification that God Is.

And in His verification of me do I verify and proclaim His Reality. As a Savior I am beset with the divine obligation to save the world. The absolute responsibility is mine to lift the burden of death from man or, since the earth is death, to awaken him wholly to his innate sense of eternity. There is nothing on earth to substantiate my Christhood.

For just a single moment in all of time I have verified my Father, but am myself without issue.

I am born but yet barren.

My true creations must at that moment through faithfulness, substantiate me in order to awaken to their own Saviorship.

It is always initially astonishing to a newly awakened Master to discover that the manner in which he thinks has undergone a radical transformation.

His former limited consciousness construct finally had nothing to do with the complete exposé. He stands naked with his own certainty. He has lost the capacity for specific comparison. The wholeness of his thinking inevitably makes the objective rationale of limited consciousness seem absurd.

He is thrust into the position of seeing that his former value system, based on specific conclusions arrived at by comparison and analysis, has no validity or even reality. He finds himself in an illogical, unreasonable place. He must now deal with his absolute, unqualified certainty that the objectively constructed world is totally meaningless, except to the necessity of bringing about the revelation that established his own transcending consciousness.

He is alone, awake among the sleeping.

Imagine, if you can, that you have made what appears to be the most stupendous, blundering mistake that could ever happen in a particular situation.

And yet you find yourself with absolutely no memory of any specific past occurrences that would in any way justify the present situation.

You are exposed

You are revealed

You are laid bare

You are defenseless

You have become magnificently vulnerable.

You discern in one glorious exposé that no justification is necessary or even possible.

You have become innocent and so by your very nature find your earthly cohorts not guilty.

It is impossible for you to understand what I am absolutely certain of because my state of mind cannot be reached by knowledge. If you wish, then, to gain freedom it is imperative that you evolve a structure of consciousness that absolutely involves a continuing process of thought that allows for no distraction and is finally, very singularly, unqualified determination to escape death and remember eternity.

If you will use me as part of your concerted effort to overcome, I assure you I will have been of inestimable value to you.

Strange as it may seem, it is necessary that I make my message complicated in some regards, or the fractured imagery you call self - in your dream - could not hear me at all. Since you are devious by your own conception we must lead you to the light of truth by your own devious route.

Because of the manner in which you think, you are inevitably perplexed by simplicity. The simpler it becomes the more perplexing. You end up trying to express the simple truth in very complicated fashions.

Total truth is incomprehensible to you by the very nature of its simplicity. Nothing is more difficult for your self-constructed identity than the idea of a complete wholeness or singularity that includes your thoughts about it. Truth is True and nothing else is True. When you awaken from this dream you'll laugh out loud at the idea of separate or relative truths.

Come then and reason with me. I awaken you now as you instructed me to do, long ago, when time began and ended.

You suffer from a single all-encompassing disease. You have a bad case of "WORLDLINESS". You must admit to the disease because it actually is your total state of mind. All consciousness on earth is a continuing adjustment to the inevitability of termination.

Your choice is finally only between various forms of disease and death! How painfully futile. As the absolute craziness of this situation becomes more and more obvious to you, you may well develop a case of "GODLINESS". You usually treat it with nostrums of false reality. World consciousness must protect itself from someone with a bad case of the "GODLIES" even to the drastic remedy of crucifixion.

Remember that the world's only remedy for GODLINESS is finally death. You persistently prescribe it for yourself and others when the threat of love becomes too pervasive. It's OK to have a little GODLINESS, as long as it remains treatable. Remember though, that death is your natural state and that you must finally, at any cost, defend yourselves from love and eternal freedom.

The world is a "Mutual Resistance Pact" designed to defend the separate self from the wholeness of truth and love.

As advanced teachers of Truth attempt to extend this message, they discover that the world is populated by a species known as

"YES-BUT-ERS."

It is fundamental to limited consciousness that there are exceptions to Truth.

If you continue with your Socratic adventure, you force the limitation to a disclaimer of his true self – as in "I'm not ready to hear that yet."

He has grown to a –

"NOT-YET-ER."

He literally will express –

"I would rather die than embrace the simple truth of my own invulnerability."

There is great joy in the kingdom with the evolvement of a –

"ONE EYER."

He is grievously offended by his own limitation and is in a constant state of –

"OTHER EYE PLUCKING."

His determination inevitably invokes a single response –

"WELCOME HOME"

When one admits to continuing foolishness he is expressing a state of mind in a high reach of clarity.

Truth is an absolute abstraction.

A consciousness in a state of advanced maturation loses the necessity and even capacity for sequential thought.

It can no longer identify itself in cause and effect relationships.

Its actions become genuinely non-motivated.

The idea that the past has nothing reasonably to do with the present makes no sense to a linear space-time rationale.

In fact, a human definition of rank foolishness would be to find itself in a situation where it could not establish correlating antecedents of thought.

A natural man, then, eventually and inevitably will find a spiritual man foolish.

And finally nothing is more foolish to natural man than a complete commitment to <u>Absolute Truth</u>.

There is a continuing tendency for spiritual teachers to give specific credence to apparently separate contingencies in the process of transformation. These include giving value to their own teaching mechanisms and judging them by comparison to be superior in particular regards to other specific methods. Methods are always of man, never of God.

The notion of method is a mind constriction. All conceptions each moment are either a denial of or an assertion of a single Truth, or singularity. No method in reality is any more beneficial than any other, except by your own observation or limited definitions. Every apparent situation in every moment of your karma history contains the total possibility or necessity for transcendence.

To all so-called therapists:

You are confirming your death process by the specific application of your limited mind construct. If all opinions you have about yourself are false, and I assure you they are, why do you give more credence to some of them than others? Once and for all, Teachers of God, the opinions you have about yourself, or your teachings, have no validity. It is time you accepted the certainty that Truth has nothing to do with your idea about it. All of your thoughts are unreasonable because your idea about yourself is unreasonable. You will never succeed in making the unreal real.

You have become in your self-consciousness a big bundle of irresolution. These unresolved dilemmas keep cropping up to hurt you. They form the basis for all the defense mechanisms you have constructed as barriers to Truth. They all stem from a basis of fundamental denial of your own singular reality.

The notion of the absolute reality of a single Truth or Universal Consciousness is not in any way therapeutic to mankind. How ridiculous the notion that discovering the Truth is therapeutic to limited consciousness. It is just the opposite. If you insist on defining yourself as a therapist, remember that all disease is one singular unreasonable thought, and there is no thought outside of your own.

To Advanced Teachers

The notion of spiritual communication, that is, mutual self-recognition occurring in conceptual duality, must involve the possibility of non-specific deferential self-expression. Since objectivity precludes communication by its very nature, we, as awakened consciousnesses, are left with the inevitable imperative of teaching singular subjective reality. Listen to me – there is absolutely no alternative to this!

What advanced teachers must finally come to realize is that giving value to "divided function" is absolutely illogical. Limited goals are no goals at all. How could there be reality in limitedness? It's the whole basis for the crazy idea there can be truly separate things or ideas. Nothing is real without communication. The idea of partial communication is absolutely irrational. Creation is the extension or self-expression of the whole truth.

Be certified by the certainty of your uncertainty.

Master teachers never prophesy. They are certain that all prophecies are self-fulfilling.

Student: Master, you told us that eating asparagus was good for the urinary system. It makes my urine green and smelly.

Master: The last thing I would tell you to do is eat asparagus.

The real problem with so-called master/student relationships is the idea of <u>intention</u>.

The problem you are encountering is you have given me intentions. You really believe that I am capable of doing something intentionally. Intentions justify action which is always limited — we are back to the notion of unmotivated action again!

Action sustains intention, as intentions justify actions; or the reverse.

Actions sustain limited intentions, which define death.

      MOTIVATED ACTION LEADS TO DEATH

What a strange malady is personality.

It is a sense of limited consciousness that instigates conceptual objectivity from which it subsequently defends itself.

Discriminate action leads to death.

All judgment is an assertion of an unreal selfness.

The basic tenet of what I know in Truth begins with the acknowledgment that the earth is not repairable.

Complete understanding is the certainty that there is nothing to be understood.

Limited understanding defines misunderstanding by its very nature.

Limited consciousness is an imposition to Truth.

It assumes a position that is alien to the whole.

Truth cannot be reached by superimposing on the original imposition.

Since nothing can impose on Truth or Wholeness, (What could it be?) your self-position and continuing super-imposition are absolutely meaningless.

Your self-positioning as the great intruder is a COSMIC JOKE.

What a Fearful Proposition –

The structure of your universe is formulated solely on the thoughts that you have "Put out of your mind", or ones that you think you possess and will subsequently reject.

Truth has nothing to do with necessity. Necessity is indeed the mother of invention, but Truth has nothing at all to do with invention.

Truth is not manufactured.

It is Godufactured.

The problem with coming to know the Truth is not so much that you are the deny-er of it, but rather the denial itself.

The only lesson you need ever realize is that it's impossible to think separately from what you are.

God did indeed create Heaven and Earth in that Heaven and Earth are one. But the notion that God would have anything to do with the Earth as you're perceiving it is totally illogical and unreasonable.

What would Truth know of falsity.
If false is possible there is no Truth.

How could total order know of the chaotic.
If chaos is real there is no order.

Could love find itself hateful?
To hate is to deny the possibility of love.

"No, my dear brother, God has no conception of the Earth, or indeed any conception at all." Conception always precedes perception.

The whole earth is but a formulation of your limited mind construct. Here then lies the only possibility of your escape from chaos, disease, and death.

<u>You need but change your mind.</u>

What could be more self-maligning than a complete genealogy tracing your ancestral heritage to Adam.

Everything is Heredity, Including Environment

There is much to be gained by the idea that you only compete against yourself.

When properly focused it can lead to the ultimate conclusion that there is nothing outside of you or your thought about it.

Without competition, peace is inevitable.

How strange that the conception and practice of so-called good nutrition insures the inevitability of your becoming sick. <u>Remedy describes sickness and establishes its reality.</u> You can no more be partially healed than you can be partially anything.

If sickness is real there is no remedy.

How vulnerable the awakened consciousness to the corruption of sustenance through consumption, assimilation and excretion.

    I just gave the kitty a spoonful of "Meow" for breakfast, came upstairs and burped chopped liver.

Peace is not found through balance.

Equanimity is meaningless to truth.

What could be more unbalanced than the idea of balance?

How ridiculous that the alternative to aging and disease is annihilation or death. Has it ever occurred to you that the only way you finally escape disease is through becoming completely diseased?

Does choosing death to escape self-inflicted disease and pain still seem reasonable to you? Or is it that you do not believe that you do this but to yourself?

During the revolution of consciousness that is going on in you the whole idea of death or annihilation will become completely absurd.

This will make you very happy.

You will see how ludicrous the notion that you as a living, creative consciousness could actually become aged, deteriorate and die.

The need to be verified for what you are is what's keeping you from being what you are. Remember you cannot be authenticated except by God, and He did so with your creation.

Be Thankful.

Faith must always precede understanding because
Understanding is Truth — and cannot be gained by knowledge.

It is impossible to satisfy a debt.

A debt can never be satisfied (The idea of debt has nothing to do with quantity).

FORGIVENESS is the debt's only satisfaction.

Forgiving is forgetting, or the recognition that you can only give to yourself.

Imbalance is not in the ledger books, but rather in the mind.

Exchange at your peril

You always lose by gaining

You keep trying to get the better of yourself

All exchange degrades —

An exchange that both parties express as fair and equitable is one in which each party feels that he has received maximum "Best of the Deal."

Exchange establishes and maintains proof of limitation. What establishes the limited consciousness more emphatically than the expectation of return compensation for something given.

All it does is prove mortality.

The notion of sharing is the same as competing.

Partnerships are always competitive, because the idea of competition is what partnerships are.

They inevitably are designed to ration limited resources.

Faith is not arrived at by comparisons.

Perception restricts faith by definition.

Partial faith or commitment is impossible. It is not faithlessness, but unfaithfulness.

Faithlessness is impossible.

Unfaithfulness is an attempt to establish faith in limitation.

Attempting to be faithful to "God and Country" or "God and anything else" will always fail.

It is in fact being unfaithful to God.

Upholding total faith in limited capacity is sure death.

Resolutions except to God are meaningless, always egoic and limiting.

The reason the Pope is infallible is -
when he says or does apparently foolish things God takes no notice.

So neither, as the Son of God and His Brother, should you!

He is perfect,
notwithstanding your unreasonable judgment of him.

The very nature of human consciousness civilization is ontological. But see how irrational is man in his protagonism to God - as though somehow Truth would require defense from an apparent adversary.

A consciousness whose very structure is antagonistic could never realistically be an advocate of Truth.

Man ends up defending his totally meaningless ideas (idols) until he brings about his totally meaningless annihilation.

The Truth of the matter is that every apparent individual on earth simply defends his own backside and more particularly other backsides with whom he is in temporary, limited association.

You are what you value.
Your reality is established by the things you cherish.
How strange this high Truth: You finally always lose the things you cherish most because you cherish them just in order to lose them. In such a manner do you cherish death, and sustain its reality.
You slay the things you love from fear of love's return.
As long as you cherish mortality you will remain mortal.
How could the mortal know of immortality? There is no source for mortality. It has no meaning.

<u>You sustain yourself by the death of your brother</u>. By your qualified love of him do you condemn him to death along with yourself. You are determined to die and take the whole world with you. But no matter how hard you try to obliviate yourself you can never succeed. All of the continuity of space/time is your consciousness of it. Actually, you are destroying and reconstructing the earth each moment in time. You will come to see that these moments are not sequential, but rather exist continuously in your individual state of consciousness.

The importance of the admonition "Resist not Evil" is obvious as you come to see that everything about you is only your <u>thought</u> about it. You must understand that you are literally being attacked by your own ideas.

Man is a prototype of God and cannot think separately from Him.

All consciousness is finally only its own prototype.

All creation is only self-expression.

How peculiar the notion of separate selves as though a whole thing could have unidentifiable parts.

God and a Hippopotamus are not different.

They both know perfectly well what they are.

The difference between man and God is all the difference there is, and God has no idea of it.

The only difference between God and man is time. God knows not of it, but it is absolutely at man's disposal since he made it in the first place.

After man made up time in the first place, the idea of other places and times was inevitable. He was trapped in his own sequentiality.

The idea of duration and death are synonymous.

The partners of death are location and longevity.

Invulnerability is recognized only through
absolute non-defensiveness.

He who has an enemy is weak indeed.

Only the innocent can be truly non-defensive.

Therefore

Only the innocent are invulnerable.

God created you as perfectly pure as Himself.
It is impossible that you be guilty in reality.
Therefore, find your brother innocent and
attest to his eternal freedom.

Truth on earth is only <u>coming to Truth</u>.
Ecstasy comes from expectation, not
fulfillment. The higher the anticipation the
greater the whole self-fulfillment possibility,
leading directly to full enlightenment.
You will soon have the experience of
awakening in the middle of the night with
ecstatic high anticipation of the immanancy of
Eternity.

How strange that if you accept my certainty that it is impossible to die, since there is no death, it will destroy all of your hopes and plans for the future. It is quite impossible at your present consciousness level to accept the inevitability of <u>eternal</u> happiness. Your apparent security, peace of mind and happiness are structured on the premise of annihilation. You love to slay and slay to love.

Man sends his issue to be slain in the sacrificial ritual of war.

"I love you, Son; now die that I may live." Men die but by the memory of their own death. To die is to fear - to live is to love.

We are come now because it is time for you to reckon with Life. It is not death you fear, but eternity. Since you are in love with death, everything in your conception loves to die. How viciously do you attack us when we attempt to take death from your hands. We would take from you your false ideas of crucifixion, destruction and death; and leave you but with eternal love and happiness. For this do you slay us.

You end up cherishing most what you hate, for without it you would lose your identity and remember that you are only love.

Suffering is not understandable.
There is no reason for it.
In truth death is not understandable.
There is no reason for it.

The only thing you can possible misunderstand is <u>yourself</u> and you do that with <u>malice and forethought</u>.

Do not mask your uncertainty in pat responses that are nothing but the same old unreasonable conclusions.

How strange -

Duality must consider absolute singularity to be an anomaly and not thought of as part of its objective concepts. Actually, conception is a limiting interpretive function. It established and maintains duality. How unreasonable the notion of ideas with separate sources. Talk about disrupting communication! It becomes impossible.

Can separate sources express identical thoughts without becoming the same?

Wholeness is identified and finally realized by absolute common purpose.

I Think I'll Define Myself

The fashion in which I teach is absolutely <u>worthless</u>.

The methods I use are <u>meaningless</u>.

All cause you give to <u>me</u> are but your <u>own</u> effects.

<u>You alone</u> determine what <u>I am</u> and what <u>I do</u>.

<u>I am</u> and will forever be <u>as you desire me</u>.

<u>In truth I have no qualifications whatever</u>.

The Text of "A COURSE IN MIRACLES" stands at this moment in space/time as a singular incomparable masterpiece (naturally, being a piece by the Master) among the ongoing incursions of harmony, love and truth into the chaos, darkness and death of the conceptual schism that is world consciousness.

"A COURSE IN MIRACLES" is so superbly dialectic that it defies comparison. Its references are boundless. The beginning lessons in the workbook represent the quintessence of the dialectic process.

Revelation is not reciprocal.

Your relationship with Truth in no way involves reciprocity. What could be more blasphemous to God, or in reality to yourself, than to ask Him for a favor? You keep trying to make a deal with Truth. You are playing a losing game. You keep trying to bet what you <u>have</u> against what He <u>Is</u>. You end up with nothing and He still is Everything. To have is only TO BE.

The Universe holds no secrets.

The whole basis for your self-identity is what you think are private thoughts.

They are literally unreal. Reality and communication are the same, they are what creation is.

The idea of partial communication is senseless.

Your earth is established to prevent communication, and deny your total creativity.

Saying "I don't know what Truth is" is simply a <u>denial</u> that "Truth Is".

It is a decision not to know, more particularly a decision not to know yourself.

Separate goals are impossible. Apparent various or variety of purposes are always illusionary.

Advice to Practicing Masters:

If you find yourself in a strange village with a bunch of Pharisees playing "Let's trap the Master," it's fine to fall back on the old "Render Unto Caesar what is Caesar's" escape. Leave them then with their continuing false impression that you have given value to Caesar.

Remember though, reality rests on your certainty that to render to "Caesar what is Caesar's" means to give nothing to nothing, and to hold on to fear and death.

No one on earth who remembers being whole, even for an instant, would ever think of constructing a limited God.

You don't really deny God, but rather <u>are</u> the denial.

How strange that denial is not a condition of limited consciousness, but <u>Is</u> limited consciousness.

All it really denies is what it has falsely constructed.

Denying the Christ

No one has attested to my fraudulency more emphatically than the entities that constitute the so-called religious establishments of the world. They proclaim and project an insidious limited advocacy that is in reality a rigorous denial.

An advanced teacher of truth tricks the awakening mind into thinking it can repair itself until it passes the consciousness point of no return.

The so-called evolutionary process is simply the increasing of the range of choices contained within the limited consciousness.

The goal of the atonement or awakening instruction is to teach the limited consciousness that its choices are absolutely limitless, and in this manner eliminate the necessity to choose.

The idea of unlimited choice, while admittedly untruthful, is actually a fine manner in which the untrue can awake to reality.

The only other possible manner is to pound the limited identity to the point where it sees in reality it has no choice at all.

Teach the sleeping consciousness to broaden its self-identity to the point where you can walk directly into his dream sequencing.

Separate goals are impossible.

We give temporary credence to your own self doubt that expresses itself in the possibility of alternatives. This is only a teaching mechanism. You have evolved a perceptual reality absolutely based on a limited self-conception. We must use that conception as a vehicle to enlightenment.

As a visitor from total time/space, will someone in this ludicrous misadventure of sequential consciousness please explain to me what the word "ultimately" means? Take your time —

Upon your awakening, the practice of self identity through apparent mutual conceptual relationships, what you called "being human", will appear tragically ludicrous.

How ridiculous the adage:

"Power corrupts and absolute power corrupts absolutely."

Nonsense – what would absolute power corrupt? Itself?

The notion of "degrees" of power is meaningless and defines weakness.

At the Masters' Academy a "tour of duty on earth" is called: "Doing a hitch in a hatchery".

"Sure enough. This morning I opened a fresh carton of eggs, and found myself tapping gently on the shells, calling, "can you hear me – can you hear me? Time to wake up." "

Actually, "Humans are more like 'PODS' than 'EGGS'."

How poverty stricken is the rich man of earth.

His wealth is used but to describe his weakness and vulnerability.

What more surely affirms deprivation than the idea of abundance!

It would obviously be difficult for a consciousness with a rigid concept of God or an inflexible doctrine in regard to truth to experience a mind transformation.

Certainly you can see that concepts or doctrines or finally value systems of any kind on earth represent a constricted self-identity.

<u>AIR   WATER   FIRE   EARTH</u>

<u>ENERGY EXPRESSED AS PHENOMENA</u>

First you walk on the earth.
Next you walk on the fire.
Then you walk on the water.
Then you walk on the air.

Then you don't walk at all because you're already there.

You have a limiting notion that when you remember you are everywhere you'll have <u>no</u> place to go.

On the contrary, when you discover you are everywhere, you will have <u>every</u> place to go.

The expression "Don't throw out the baby with the bath water" expresses very well the limited persona's determination to hold on to unreality. You are never going to get your "baby" clean. Its corruption but describes your state of mind.

Finally, the process is simple. If you feel you must scrub the "baby" first, go ahead. Then throw out the bath water, then throw out the "baby". Obviously then, you'll have no use for the tub, so throw that out too.

There would never be a need to scrub the Christ Child, would there!

All Master Teachers finally and inevitably teach subjective reality.

In this sense the objective world must consider the absolute uncompromising teachings of a supra-consciousness to be a direct threat to its very existence. And so it is. What a situation! As a teacher of Truth you're a menace to the world. The higher and more subjectively demanding the reaches of your teaching, the more threatening you become.

The absolute basis for all so called "Secret" spiritual or occult organizations on earth has always been to protect the Master (that is, the Word of God.)

The very nature of the entire establishment of the earth is antagonistic to a Whole Truth. (If you could find the Christ, you'd kill him and do so each moment in your limited self-conception.)

Face it – the teachings of all Cosmic Truth Ambassadors, from the view point of a separated sociological system, are interpreted as advocating anarchy and as such are a threat to all earth establishments.

It is very difficult for a Master Teacher to "hang out" the "Greater Mysteries" let alone the "Greatest Mystery of All".

Yet, suddenly here I am caught inexorably in an attempt to do so.

Actually we drew straws at the Masters Academy, and I drew the shortest one!

NEWS BULLETIN

There's wonderful news from the "Let's All Practice Forgiveness" Group of A Course In Miracles in Selroy, California. The group leader Ms. Margarette L.L. Thurston II reports that at their last regular meeting a member successfully, and much to the delightful astonishment of all, whistled *The Marseillaise* out of a portion of his rear anatomy. Group members, George and Alma Finstly pledged to "really get out there and 'Forgive' in earnest" this week. He's a bass and she's an alto. They are determined to form a trio and whistle "Hark the Herald Angels Sing" by Christmas. Good luck Miracle Workers!

The whole civilization of man is just an oil slick on the King's Highway.

What is a black hole to earth's astronomers is actually a leak in the crank case of an old cosmic communicator's 36 Studebaker.

How can you win or lose when you are only
battling your own false condition.

Thoughts do not lead to conclusions.
They are the conclusions and attempt to
represent them.

Do not represent yourself falsely.
You have been a liar from the beginning.

Do not represent yourself at all.
Everything you think about yourself is untrue
and has never been and will never be.

Remember you can never think <u>about</u>
anything. And that most implicitly, includes
yourself.

This may be difficult, but the truth is, you
really don't have any emotions at all.

Remember, that, if you <u>have</u> the emotion, you
ARE the emotion.

High Thoughts –

Almost nothing is more unreasonable or illogical to an awakened mind than the concept that Time is Sequential.

The persona's determination for self-identity based on previous experience makes no sense at all to an awakened mind. In the case of the destruction of the American space shuttle – when world mind announces that the shuttle explosion was caused by a defective fuel tank, awakened mind is immediately aware that, on the contrary, it is the explosion of the shuttle which caused the booster tanks to be defective. An awakened mind is fully aware that conception must precede perception. If you base present occurrences on past experiences, you are thinking only in the past tense. This is what linear time thinking is. In reality a billion to one chance of an occurrence is exactly as likely to happen as a one to one chance. Cause and effect are never apart. If you can think of it, it is and was and will be. This is not in any way to indicate that space/time does not have continuity; that is, that it is not a whole single thing.

On the contrary, your beingness is based on continuity of mind. But that continuity is absolutely not sequential unless your limited state of consciousness is determined to make it so.

Yes, Brother Albert (Einstein), God as you conceive of him does indeed roll dice!

God's Will has no intention, nor is it in anyway disciplined.

Nothing could ever be ultimately more chaotic to you than God's Will.

The closest the limited consciousness can get to real thought is the notion of statistical possibility or chance. Since real thought has no antecedent at all (that is, it is not sequential), the limited consciousness must finally arrive at the inevitable conclusion that the whole universe is random.

And indeed it is.

The idea that God, or truth or unqualified wholeness would in any way require order or discipline is nonsense.

There is an adventurous soul at Carnegie-Mellon who is attempting to discover a so-called <u>process of scientific thinking</u>. This is a lovely example of upside down backward thinking. He provides a computer the same conceptual data that the astronomer Kepler ostensibly had when he formulated the third law of planetary motion. When the computer arrives at Kepler's conclusions, he proclaims that it has <u>discovered</u> something.

Nonsense! If you feed the same computer the ingredients of a jar of Chef Boyardee it will discover spaghetti sauce. The fundamental flaw in this adventure in fractured reasoning is the notion that any real or whole thing or idea, expressed objectively, is the sum of the parts that in retrospect have given it its' apparent reality. All <u>real</u>, so-called, scientific discoveries are actually <u>creations</u>. They are dramatic demonstrations of the innate capability of mind to assemble previously dissociated conceptions into a <u>whole new</u> and inevitably more <u>unified</u> relationship. It is not only <u>new</u>, but it changes the concepts of its <u>parts</u> as well. The discoverer is expressing a manner of whole mind thinking or recognizing that, in time, invariably leads to an exposé of a totally presumptive à priori singularity of consciousness.

We absolutely guarantee the gentleman that his computer or any other contraption of objectivity is nothing more than a projection of his own self-identity. His sense of reality is established on it. And it will finally tell him or show him exactly what he does or does not want to hear or see in verification of that reality.

So much for so-called scientific inventiveness, and a noble undertaking it was.

Here is the inevitable dilemma - virtually all consciousness on earth while in a state of continuing maturation or evolution is nevertheless most specifically retrospective. Its apparent reality in space/time is established on the illogical conclusion that cause and effect are particularly sequential, or in truth sequential at all. The assertion or assumption that there were specific objective ideas or occurrences that brought about the discovery of the third law of planetary motion is no more logical than that the idea of a planetary motion law engendered the ideas of the data and occurrences that apparently brought it about.

It was an early Spring morning on the outskirts of Prague. The year was 1608 and the Imperial Mathematician was tired and discouraged. He had spent most of the night in the open, observing the Red Wanderer in the sky, and did not relish returning home to a melancholy spouse and hounding creditors.

First light had appeared and a new day was dawning as a gentle April shower began to fall. He lifted his face and let the soft patter gladden his red-rimmed eyes; then sought shelter in an abandoned thatch roof barn close by.

"There's a way to measure God's order" he mused as he settled in the hay. "Out there it's not finally different than here. I'm sure of it". He glanced up as a sudden shaft of sunlight exploded over the horizon and beamed through a hole in the roof above bathing the room in a golden glow. There between two rafters glistening brightly with droplets of rain shimmered a finely spun spider web.

He stared intensely for an <u>eternal moment</u> - then "That's it", he exclaimed excitedly. "That's it of course."

Getting quickly to his feet he headed for the city to commit his <u>new discoveries</u> to writing and to pacify the clamoring bill collectors as best he could.

We understand that conceptual consciousness is based on the continuity of ideas emanating from mind in apparent cause and effect relationships.

If you insist, however, on relating them sequentially, your mind will be forever held captive in the necessity of maintaining a limited form of apparent reality based on a past genetic retrospective recall that in truth has nothing at all to do with your present state of consciousness. You are held in the bondage of time exactly by the notion of sequentiality or the distance between cause and effect.

The Truth that cause and effect can never be apart comes with recognition that only your limited self-establishment stands between them. You have invented time and it is absolutely at your disposal. It is important to remember, however, that the act of creating, unlike inventing, is not sequential and there is nothing potential about eternity.

All creative thinking really involves is the certainty of possibility.

If you think you can break off a HUNK FROM WHOLE TRUTH, you must end up with:

1) two pieces, neither of which is TRUTH (impossible) or

2) a WHOLE TRUTH with a piece of UNTRUTH (impossible) or

3) two pieces of WHOLE TRUTH

How easy to see that nothing could be separated from WHOLE TRUTH.

It must be then that the part of you that thinks it is separate is UNREAL.

The Theology of Thomas Altizer (God is Dead) presents the Truth in virtually the most untruthful manner in which it may be presented. Total untruth is impossible but its attempted proclamation is the closest unreal or limited consciousness construct can get to singular reality.

The second highest statement that can be made, in an attempt to describe a singular reality, is "Everything is untrue, nothing is true". The highest statement then becomes and must be: "Everything is true, nothing is untrue".

The second highest statement is absolutely uncreative and represents <u>death</u>.

The highest statement is absolutely creative and is <u>life</u>.

Untruth is aware of Truth and considers it to be a part of its untruthfulness. Obviously, Truth has no awareness of untruth whatsoever.

Having an awareness of Truth makes it untruthful.

The highest thought that objective consciousness can have or express is "Everything is nothing". It does so, and then proceeds to search for something more than the nothing it proclaims to be everything. It quite literally tries to express or possess more than everything, only to discover that its more than everything is still nothing.

Tell me, Dear Brother, Why <u>have</u> the message "Everything is Nothing", when in reality you <u>are</u> the message that "Everything is Everything".

In the science of statistical probability the wholeness of the Universe is "<u>POSSIBILITY ONE</u>" which means that it is eternally inevitable.

<u>Everything happens by its mere possibility</u>.

> In earth consciousness –
> Death is Probability One.

The Weatherman

Once upon a time at a small TV station in a medium-sized town in the Mid-Western United States there was a weatherman. He was a competent meteorologist and after studying national weather bureau data and other local sources would appear nightly on television and, as accurately as most forecasters, predict the weather conditions.

One night, to his amazement, a miraculously beautiful spiritual vision overcame him. He was shown the total unity of purpose of man in his search for truth. He saw that God is - and through the revelation recognized that he had the power to make absolute and inevitably perfect predictions.

Deciding to test his newly acquired talent, on the 6:00 weather the following night, he forthrightly made the incredible prediction that beginning at the end of his broadcast and for a 24 hour period, no precipitation of any kind would fall on the earth. Not rain, not snow, not sleet, not hail, not anything, not anywhere. And sure enough the miracle happened. Hour after hour passed and as the deadline approached all reporting stations confirmed the total absence of moisture of any kind. The earth trembled at the prospect of perfection. Fortunately, at the last moment, a flock of high flying birds plopped on a Bulgarian wheat farmer. The weatherman immediately became the target of intense criticism, was attacked, derided and scorned and forced to resign from the station.

Three days later, rejected, despondent and friendless, he was run over by a taxi in downtown Cleveland and killed.

Following his death his near perfect prediction became legend. And his martyrdom verified, he was proposed for Sainthood and canonized in record time.

He is known as the Soothsaying Saint and is venerated as the patron of Fortune Tellers, Clairvoyants, Religious Prophesiers, Economic Advisors, Market Analyzers, Bookmakers and of course Weatherpersons.

The problem is not that the Universe is _many_ dimensional, but that it is _any_ dimensional. Any concept of dimension at all must extrapolate to objectivity or duality.

You are constructed in a posture of reasoning where infinity is subtracted from the so-called scientific process.

Finally the single anomaly that must forever exist for finite mind reasoning is infinity. It is, however, an absolute probability that finite or limited thought (what you might call activated potential) will reach a conclusion of a finite infinity.

The notion of an infinitely finite universe is as close as conceptual thought can get to non-conceptional singularity.

The new "string theory" about the formulation of a single universal law for everything involves a very lucid form of reasoning.

Time is the distance between cause and effect.

Time and space appear to be the same idea since one is not possible without the other. In reality Time is the causation and space the effect.

Time is the notion of "event".

Space is the "event" manifested.

Space is congruent Time or event.

Self-identity in Space/Time is the continuity of congruent events.

The closer the cause to the effect the less linearly sequential the continuity of time.

<u>Time is not sequential.</u>

The idea of motion does not have to do with movement.

Think of motion as consciousness itself with light as an aspect of that consciousness.

Motion then can be seen as a continuing act of extension without object.

Absolute wholeness or stillness is a state of unqualified motion.

Time is established by qualified motion (or acceleration).

Remember that in its intrincity everything is the same speed (its own).

There is no reality in relationship (relativity).

What we are defining is creation which is continuing Eternity.

There is no such thing as potential.

It is activated by the very thought of it.

Who has a more deterministic idea about chance than Prigogine and Stengers (Order out of Chaos) or for that matter has a more chancy determinism.

The idea that apparent dissipation, that is loss of equilibrium or the onset of chaos is necessary in the universal onrush to unification is indeed observedly valid (as in "no pain, no gain").

But their assertion that at the moment of maximum disorder chance would be involved in determining the state of the more unified system is unreasonable (illogical).

As a matter of fact, the whole concept of operations of increasing order is absolutely deterministic.

The idea of a synthesis between chance and necessity is dualistic silliness.

It is logically impossible that the idea of possibility (chance) and inevitability (determinism) not finally be one and the same thought.

Determinism and free will are the same idea as cause and effect.

Determinism is cause - Free will is effect.

Free will is the effect of determinism which is its cause.

Free will is the absolute total possibility to be effective.

You are determined to be effective but not totally so.

Your idea of freedom is bondage to limited causation.

Your idea of bondage is the freedom of total causation.

Cause and effect are never apart.

Determination and free will are one singular everlasting event.

The gap between cause and effect you call <u>time.</u>

It has established your perceptual universe.

Determinism and Free Will

Determinism is the absolute capacity to be everything.

Free will is the absolute capacity to be everything.

A hippopotamus is not everything because it thinks it is everything but rather because it thinks.

The limitation of species man places on a hippo concerns it not in the least.

A human is determined that a hippo suffers from a case of hippoism only because he is sick with a case of humanness.

While it is true that the world is a state of mind, that is not to say that any state of mind is true.

Indeed, since you have a state of mind, and all states of mind are false, the world you think you see is inevitably false.

How utterly simple and logical the assertion that "Reality is not conditional". It shines with blazing clarity from an illuminated mind, yet to a perceptual self-determined consciousness it is an unfathomable enigma.

It appears to theologians as though there is a conflict between determinism (what you call the inevitability of everything) and free will (which apparently gives you choice in what you think or what actions you take.) Actually, all earth consciousness is not an assertion, but rather a denial of free will. In reality, your will is absolutely unlimited and the limitations you place upon it are what bind you to the extermination process – that is aging and death. You suffer pain, are diseased and die by your own decision.

There is no alternative to your finally discovering that this must be true.

Your true nature, that is, what you are, is what the Will of God is, and it is absolutely determined that you are as free as your Father. There is no alternative to free will because it is what universal consciousness is.

This has nothing at all to do with what you think God is. It is the simple acknowledgment of a single source.

Determinism and free will are the single truth. Determinism is the cause, free will the effect. They are never apart. When we attest that universal mind is singular, we mean that literally. It is a single state of beingness. It is all that you are and you are all that it is.

How strange that the final anomaly in all so-called scientific thought is always the thinker.

A spiritually maturing consciousness will inevitably have a strong necessity to establish and often proclaim its antecedents. The whole idea of a spiritual path is in reality nothing more than an attempt to identify and validate self-consciousness. Is there anyone in the world with the discernment to see that the admonition: "Know Yourself" or "To thine own self be true" is paradoxical?

Knowledge cannot be gained by your perceptions and is most certainly not conceptional. That's the whole dilemma. You actually believe you can have a conception of yourself, or selfness.

>To <u>know</u> yourself is to <u>be</u> yourself.

>To <u>conceive</u> is to <u>have</u> an idea.

>To <u>create</u> is to <u>be</u> an idea.

It is impossible for you to <u>have</u> or to <u>make</u> anything.

It is possible for you to <u>be</u> and to <u>create</u> everything.

You are not what you <u>think you are</u>, but only what <u>you think</u>.

All the separate ones let what they think establish what they think they are.

Thinking that leads to conclusions is not really thinking at all.

When you are angry you are all the anger there is.

You can no more have an emotion than you can have anything.

You are what you feel, not what you think you feel.

You are not an establishment.

When you are happy you are all the happiness there could ever be.

True self is not conditional because truth has no condition.

It cannot be constructed on various so-called conditions of your mind.

You are never angry, but only anger.

You are not fearful, but rather fear.

When you think you can die, you do not really represent the cause of death, you are Death itself.

Your love is what the universe is, and all that it is.

Subjective reality is nothing but a state of unconditionalness.
Objectivity is the state of being conceptional.
Unconditionality is obviously non-conceptional.
The highest truth that "To have is to be"' is defined thus:

"To <u>have</u> is always conditional"

"To <u>be</u> is always unconditional"

Since certainty lies only in "being", you must give everything you <u>have</u> in order to <u>be</u>.

As long as you <u>have</u> something, you can never <u>be real</u> -

Beingness is not a state of anything.

What a weird idea is expressed in Eastern Yoga traditions - that you can reach a state of unconditional consciousness!
Who can reach it?

It will become increasingly obvious to you that you are responsible for your own thoughts and cannot escape the consequences of them.

For indeed, the consequences are contained in the very thought and are finally what the thought is.

Awakened Mind: You know everything.

Human Mind: Nonsense, there are lots of things that I don't know.

AM: What are they?

HM: I don't know.

AM: What?

HM: I say, I don't know.

AM: Don't know what?

HM: How do I know, I don't know it!

AM: What is it you don't know?

HM: I told you I don't know.

AM: Do you know what you know?

HM: Of course.

AM: Then it must be that you know what you don't know.

HM: No I don't.

AM: What do you mean?

HM: I don't know what it is I don't know, but I do know that I don't know it.

AM: They told me this would be a tough assignment, but this is ridiculous.

HM: What did you say?

AM: Never mind, let's try again.

AM: Are you ready for this?

HM: Try me.

AM: What you don't know isn't.

HM: What are you saying?

AM: I'm saying that all you can think of is all that there is.

HM: (pause) Are you telling me that anything I can't think of isn't anything?

AM: Now you're getting it.

A very difficult concept for an identity in self construct is the determination that the idea of "not knowing" or lack of knowledge, is a decision.

The decision to "know" something involves precisely the same thought process as "not knowing".

In the process of reasoning to truth, that is the practice of coming to wholeness, the admonition "know thyself" is certainly no more to the mark than "don't know thyself"!

You are perched on your own limitation limb. What a dilemma. While it is impossible to know yourself, it is equally impossible not to know yourself.

Rather, only "be yourself" each moment in time. By doing so, you will be and were re-cognized and brought to fruition.

<u>Having</u> an idea has nothing at all to do with the idea itself.

The incredible distance between Hegel and Kierkegaard's attempts to define self is very obvious here. While they both appear to be existentialists, the difference between their rationale is the exact distance between chaos and order (enlightenment). There is a gap between Hegel's cause and effect. Very few human minds can as yet accept with certainty the universal truth that <u>TO HAVE IS TO BE</u>. Yet this is what enlightenment is.

It is finally the only manner that death can awaken to eternity.

While he is never able to articulate it fully, Kierkegaard is in vehement opposition to Hegel because he intuits that Hegel's authenticity of self consciousness (existentialism) inevitably dissipates to dualistic anarchy, as a false alternative to the reality of the singular anarchy that is Man and God (transcendent existentialism).

Giordano Bruno has no such problem with the Aristotelian peripatetics.

He annihilates their illogical dualistic determinations with a singular resolution and divine irony that emanates from a transcendent certainty of mind.

Oh Shut up!

"HAVING" separates cause and effect.
"BEING" brings them together.

"HAVING" establishes space and time.
"BEING" is eternal.

"Having" is cause.
"Being" is effect.
Cause and effect can never be apart.
Having and being can never be apart.
Cause is effect. Being is having.

We will define death as the distance between what you <u>think</u> and what you <u>think you are</u>.
The statement I AM has nothing to do with what you are.
"Forgive them for they know not what they do" has nothing to do with what they did.

Being what you <u>are</u> in no way requires that you set any standards at all for what you <u>need be</u>.

<u>Self-identity</u> has nothing to do with identifying the <u>self</u>.

Enlightenment is a wedding of what you think you are with what you think.

What you <u>are</u> in reality has nothing to do with your ideas about yourself. True ideas are not <u>about</u> anything, but rather about everything.

Will somebody please tell me whether the title "Your Holiness" means "Your Fullness" or "Your Emptiness"?

How delicious the notion that a person with high status in the strange spiritual hierarchies of human religious establishment would be called, "Your Emptiness"!

Wow – That would be progress brother, real spiritual progress.

What could be more senseless or illogical to an Awakened Mind than the idea of atrophy.

If you must think of the Universe as winding down think of it as winding down to everything.

Then practice winding yourself down to the personal discovery that you are that everything.

All so called scientific "disciplines" are attempts to express the undisciplined. In a very real sense the universe, as conceptional reason must finally define it, will appear totally undisciplined.

The idea of an ordered truth or wholeness is unreal.

In reality God is not mandatory!

There is a great deal of value in obstention, whether in thought or action, most particularly if it is done unreservedly and without motivation. The arguments for or against any form of self fullness or indulgences are inevitably one-sided. The scales are always weighted on the side of self-indulgence.

<u>Purity need not be justified and cannot finally be.</u>

<u>There is no reason for Truth.</u>

Holiness (or Wholiness) is self-evident. There is nothing comparable to it. Cause and effect are one. The value of obstention is in the act of obstaining not in the justification of it. All acts are self-justifying.

Relative position is no position. There is no reality in justified action. Attaching previous causation to apparent present circumstances establishes objective sequentiality or space/time. Objective thought is without cause, and therefore meaningless.

"It occurs to me that I keep saying the same thing over and over and over and over and over and bla bla bla bla bla bla bla..."
"The hell with it!"
"See you in a hundred years."

"Well here we are back again."
"Now about the case for subjective reality........"

One more time -

Order is not an alternative to chaos. It is the natural simple state of wholeness that has no alternatives.

Uncertainty and choice are the same idea.
Uncertainty is the cause.
Choice is the effect.
They are never separated.
How fearful the prospect of real alternatives.

Good is not an alternative to evil.
Wholeness is not an alternative to partiality.
Perfection is not an alternative to defection.
Light is not an alternative to darkness.
Truth is not an alternative to falsity.
God is not an alternative to man.

From a Master Communicator's point of view, accelerating the birth of an advanced embryo consciousness that is configurated in the manner of the earth within the energy fabric of the whole space/time continuum is a very sensitive undertaking. You may think of it as using forceps in the birth canal. We are attempting to assist the birth of enlightenment without crushing the skull.

Can you hear this –

Everything that you're apparently thinking about right now will all ready have been.

The very most credit you can give the past is that it is gone.

Does it not seem strange to you that you attempt to base your whole self formulation on apparent events that are gone forever? How can your present effects be real if they have no cause? By the very necessity of cause and effect you past tense your future and cover now which is really the only time there is.

Now here's the weirdest event of all.

Since the pain, disease and stress of self creation (that is self conceived sequential time) eventually becomes unbearable, you have, within your own genetic memory codes constructed your own annihilation.

Listen to me, "There is no such thing as death".

Coming to enlightenment or awakening is a process of <u>selective memory</u> that eventually eliminates or refines all specific previous memories that hold you in the bondage of limited self conception.

Let's present it as simply as possible.

The exact difference between a limited concept of self mind (man) and an awakened whole mind (Master) is that a whole mind has no need to establish a concept of itself.

Isn't it obvious that the whole problem is your need to ask the question: "What am I?" and attempt to find an answer?

To many of you now in this accelerated program of awakening, the absurdity of the observation and admission that not a single human being on earth really knows what he is, where he is, where he came from, or where he's going and nothing at all about himself in relationship to the Universe that is apparently all around him, is becoming more and more intolerable.

Make no mistake about it. The place where you are apparently configurated in your limited self-identity is totally chaotic and well defined as insane. To be conscious self, which is what the Universe is, and then pretend you're not, and attempt to establish a different separate identity is sheer madness.

What finally becomes more complex than definitions of simplicity.

All doctrine is an attempt to define the undefinable, and identifies it falsely in the very attempt.

The earth is nothing but a mass false doctrine. It is the notion there could be reality in separate things that would subsequently require definition.

The rose is not in competition with the weed.

Conflict in reality is impossible.

But how joyful the excruciating certainty of Total Love.

How intense the friction of creation.

In music, how lovingly harmonious the competition of a diminished seventh chord.

The apparent competition of Reality expresses itself in beauty.

Each song is a whole hymn to Truth and is joyously appreciated and gratefully honored by the competitors.

How glorious the victory of your adversary in Truth.

How grateful we are to our God Committed Brother!

Happiness is richly contained in anticipation.
<u>EXPECT GOD NOW!</u>

The same can be said for LOVE.
<u>EXPECT LOVE NOW!</u>

Keep your wicks trimmed.

Keep your lamps filled.

He cometh as thief in the night.

In the Darkest Night of your Soul.

In the dim desolation of your Gethsemane.

When all of your disciples still sleep.

When your God is deaf to your cry to remove the cup.

When your final desperate demand to know "Why God has forsaken you?" echoes across an empty Universe.

Then the time of your awakening is at hand.

You are constructing in your individual passion the drama of resurrection.

Ah! But now with a difference.

This time you're the central character.

This time at last, you play the leading part.

Fulfilling the law as you go, marking each milestone with your healing grace, you walk the seven miles from Bethlehem to Jerusalem and are met at the place of the skull.

You know the script well for you've rehearsed every character.

You've been the soldier that rolled the dice and the one with the spear that pierced.

In one scene you've shouted "Hosanna, Hosanna" and called "Barabbas, save Barabbas" in the next.

You've denied with Peter, connived as Judas, and doubted as Thomas.

As a blind man you've seen, as a cripple you've walked. As a leper your sores have been healed.

You've puzzled as Nicodemus, pretended as Pilate and as Lazarus come forth at His call.

And now getting closer – you've played the dear virgin and pondered His birth in your heart.

At last are you shorn of – in one terrible moment – the last vestige of armour from Truth.

Now call out to God, now call out at last, the victorious shout of surrender.

"Father, into thy hands I command my whole self."

"It is finished. It is finished forever."

Up, up you arise from the tomb that is earth, impregnant with light of fulfillment.

Now the veil of your temple is rent and the dazzling beauty of your Sonship is revealed in full array.

AND NOW THE MOST EXCITING, GLORIOUS, STUPENDOUS SURPRISE THERE COULD EVER BE IN <u>ALL OF TIME</u>:

<u>YOU'RE STILL YOU.</u>

All that has happened is that you have awakened from your fearful dream of destruction and death.

The Earth is over, gone and never was.

You're home in the heaven you never left.

And every loving thought you ever had while dreaming is with you still, along with all your other eternal creations.

"<u>Heaven is all around you – SLEEPING ONES!</u>"

We teach in Truth that enlightment is a changing of your mind.

It's very important for you to remember that this is a literal, ongoing, physical, mental and emotional occurrence.

It is an actual continuing shift in your sense of reality.

I told one of my earth Christian brothers the other day that the absolute only requirement for his entrance into heaven and eternal peace and happiness was that he take all other earth beings with him.

He was appalled that I would dare even to suggest such a thing.

You will be free when you realize that total Truth, which is what God is, is absolutely non-judgmental, and in fact could never have the capacity to judge, or in reality any capacities at all except to create you perfectly.

The only things that would be lacking or missing in your human relationships are the things you don't bring to them.

Earth relationships are contrived chains of savage bondage.
The chains that bind are always only ones of guilt.
Judge all relationships by your willingness to forgive and release.
Total Love is total freedom.

Your recognition of Truth is in no way a requirement for its truthfulness.

But it is indeed a requirement for your truthfulness, for since it is all there is it must be what you are. Recognition of Truth is indeed recognition of Self.

That "Your Kingdom is not of this Earth"
is absolutely intolerable to Kingdoms of
the Earth.

It expresses the certainty of freedom
from Death.

All Earth establishments are bound by the
Death process.

All Earthlings make a bargain with Death,
one which they cannot keep, for there is no
reality in the idea of Death.

There's an old bromide often repeated at the Masters Academy that says, when you're dealing with a suddenly rapid paced consciousness maturation or mind metamorphosis as is happening on the planet earth, "THE MORE THAT AWAKEN, THE MORE THAT AWAKEN". The awakening is contagious through the communication of Love.

The <u>dis</u>ease of fear that infests the human mind actually is not communicative. It is a <u>state</u> of consciousness. That is, <u>any</u> fear is <u>all</u> fear. Terror, is finally, very lonely. Love on the other hand is a moment by moment extension or expression of a whole self that is indeed very communicative and in that sense is an "Ease" that can be literally transmitted and caught. Almost everyone has come down with a case of Love at one time or another. Being objective and judgmental and based on limited conception of self, it of course never lasts very long.

But, listen to me, the moments and memories of love are accumulative. Since love is your own creative self-expression, the more you give, the more you have. In fact the only proof of having is giving. Finally total Love is nothing but total communication.

Love is a communicative "<u>Ease</u>"

There is a fundamental intolerance of total forgiveness in the body-mind or separate-self. Since it is in a state of comparison perception, it attempts to stabilize through disorientation. Since its self-identity depends on "not understanding", direct communication is its greatest fear. You are guilty by the very ordering of your thoughts.

Isn't it obvious that attempting to communicate with a "something" that you are intentionally disassociating yourself from is real "Loonie Bin"?

Since it is impossible to love something you hate, you end up "Loving to Hate".

Limited relationships are only mutual hating.

ABOUT UNCONDITIONAL LOVE

The idea of "Unconditional Love" is not really very valuable because your whole method of thinking is conditional. Strange as it may seem, nothing is more conditional than the admonition that you must "Love Unconditionally". Students practicing Course in Miracles inevitably become highly conditional in their "Unconditional Love" attempts. The eternal paradox rears its head as perforce it must. It is the false certainty of objective consciousness that unconditionally is itself a condition. This is inevitably true since the idea of conditions is all that objective consciousness is. Objective consciousness' idea about subjectivity (unconditionality) is exactly the opposite of what it is.

What we are apparently expressing then, is that Unconditional Love is only experiential, and so it is. But, wait a minute, let's take a closer look for now we're at the crux of the problem.

Unconditional Love is not a state of Universal Consciousness, but rather what consciousness itself is. It must be then, since you are conscious, that even though you pretend not to know who you are, that <u>what</u> you are is what Total Love or Truth or God is. No matter how much you protest there is finally simply nothing else.

As an Awakened Teacher, I love you totally, very simply, because the parts about you that you think of as unlovable, have absolutely no meaning to me. I understand that you continue to think they do. In my process of Awakening, I was shown graphically and dramatically the unreality of individual entities on Earth.

In that regard, it couldn't possibly make the slightest difference to me finally what attributes you seem to possess, or kinds of credentials you have obtained to identify yourself. None of them have the slightest validity because the consciousness that uses them to establish itself is simply non-existent. I know perfectly well who you are in reality.

You are absolutely entitled to eternal happiness, joy, love and peace because that is what the universe is and therefore what you are. You are killing yourself with your "Eye for an Eye" world. There is nothing outside of your idea about it. You are being attacked by your own thoughts.

Give up responsibility for your mis-creations.

You are guilty by the very ordering of your thoughts.

Responsibility to earth is irresponsibility to God.

All of earth consciousness is nothing but "untruth" judging "untruth against untruth" –

You didn't make yourself!

I know it's very fearful to you, but come on now, considering the condition of your world, why not take a chance on forgiveness and love.

I know the process of giving up the fearful you, through finding your brother "not guilty" insults all of your rationale of justice. But finally, what alternative do you have? You can never find justice on earth because it is impossible that there be any. Come share the freedom of non-judgment and forgiveness that leads directly to the transformation of mind that is your awakening from the "dream of separation and death".

You have a tendency to allow the apparently separate entities around you to establish <u>your</u> sense of reality through <u>their</u> judgment.

They are attempting to identify themselves through a false image of you. What nonsense. All judgment is self judgment. If no one here has the slightest idea of who they are, how can they possibly judge anything else.

Remember, if you must judge, the least and most you can do is find everyone innocent.

Herein lies eternal freedom.

Will someone please tell me what's wrong with a totally non-conflictual universe?

The problem obviously is that the source of conflict is conception itself.

Perception is discretional thought. Discretion involves choice which is conflictual by definition.

Let's face it – the reason that God embarrasses you so much is that he is totally indiscreet. More than advocating free love, he's what free love *is*. There is absolutely nothing discreet about total love. That's why the idea of it is finally frightening to you. Your necessity to qualify love is killing you.

Any moment now your going to experience God's love. Talk about indiscreet!

The real reason you are fearful of a Teacher of God is going to dawn on you any second now. Are you ready!

"I herewith condemn you to Eternal Life."

Listen to me – listen carefully to me now. There is no possibility that you can or will ever be able to escape your own thought. Not ever.

I am condemning you to your own thoughts whatever they may be.

I love <u>you</u> more than anything else in the Universe.
And I mean <u>you</u> - individually.
Indeed, you <u>are</u> the whole Universe to me.
Without <u>you</u> I am hopelessly lost forever.

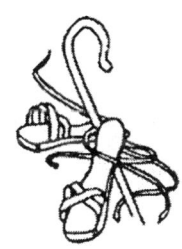

A Spiritual Teachers Notebook: High Thoughts From A Later-Day Master
Master Teacher

This Edition Published, March 2004

Published by Endeavor Academy Library
Endeavor Academy
501 East Adams Street, Wisconsin Dells WI, 53965
www.endeavoracademy.com
info@endeavoracademy.com

For a full list of publications available through
the Miracles Communication Center
please send an email to mcc@endeavoracademy.com

www.spiritualteachersnotebook.com
info@spiritualteachersnotebook.com